"This series is a tremendous resource for those war understanding of how the gospel is woven throug pastors and scholars doing gospel business from all logical feast preparing God's people to apply the entire Bible to all of life with heart and mind wholly committed to Christ's priorities."

> **BRYAN CHAPELL,** President Emeritus, Covenant Theological Seminary; Senior Pastor, Grace Presbyterian Church, Peoria, Illinois

"Mark Twain may have smiled when he wrote to a friend, 'I didn't have time to write you a short letter, so I wrote you a long letter.' But the truth of Twain's remark remains serious and universal, because well-reasoned, compact writing requires extra time and extra hard work. And this is what we have in the Crossway Bible study series *Knowing the Bible*. The skilled authors and notable editors provide the contours of each book of the Bible as well as the grand theological themes that bind them together as one Book. Here, in a 12-week format, are carefully wrought studies that will ignite the mind and the heart."

> **R. KENT HUGHES,** Visiting Professor of Practical Theology, Westminster Theological Seminary

"*Knowing the Bible* brings together a gifted team of Bible teachers to produce a high-quality series of study guides. The coordinated focus of these materials is unique: biblical content, provocative questions, systematic theology, practical application, and the gospel story of God's grace presented all the way through Scripture."

> **PHILIP G. RYKEN,** President, Wheaton College

"These *Knowing the Bible* volumes provide a significant and very welcome variation on the general run of inductive Bible studies. This series provides substantial instruction, as well as teaching through the very questions that are asked. *Knowing the Bible* then goes even further by showing how any given text links with the gospel, the whole Bible, and the formation of theology. I heartily endorse this orientation of individual books to the whole Bible and the gospel, and I applaud the demonstration that sound theology was not something invented later by Christians, but is right there in the pages of Scripture."

> **GRAEME L. GOLDSWORTHY,** former lecturer, Moore Theological College; author, *According to Plan, Gospel and Kingdom, The Gospel in Revelation,* and *Gospel and Wisdom*

"What a gift to earnest, Bible-loving, Bible-searching believers! The organization and structure of the Bible study format presented through the *Knowing the Bible* series is so well conceived. Students of the Word are led to understand the content of passages through perceptive, guided questions, and they are given rich insights and application all along the way in the brief but illuminating sections that conclude each study. What potential growth in depth and breadth of understanding these studies offer! One can only pray that vast numbers of believers will discover more of God and the beauty of his Word through these rich studies."

> **BRUCE A. WARE,** Professor of Christian Theology, The Southern Baptist Theological Seminary

KNOWING THE BIBLE

J. I. Packer, Theological Editor
Dane C. Ortlund, Series Editor
Lane T. Dennis, Executive Editor

•   •   •   •   •   •

Genesis	Psalms	Jonah, Micah, and	Ephesians
Exodus	Proverbs	Nahum	Philippians
Leviticus	Ecclesiastes	Haggai, Zechariah,	Colossians and
Numbers	Song of Solomon	and Malachi	Philemon
Deuteronomy	Isaiah	Matthew	1–2 Thessalonians
Joshua	Jeremiah	Mark	1–2 Timothy and
Judges	Lamentations,	Luke	Titus
Ruth and Esther	Habakkuk, and	John	Hebrews
1–2 Samuel	Zephaniah	Acts	James
1–2 Kings	Ezekiel	Romans	1–2 Peter and Jude
1–2 Chronicles	Daniel	1 Corinthians	1–3 John
Ezra and Nehemiah	Hosea	2 Corinthians	Revelation
Job	Joel, Amos, and	Galatians	
	Obadiah		

•   •   •   •   •   •

J. I. PACKER is Board of Governors' Professor of Theology at Regent College (Vancouver, BC). Dr. Packer earned his DPhil at the University of Oxford. He is known and loved worldwide as the author of the best-selling book *Knowing God*, as well as many other titles on theology and the Christian life. He serves as the General Editor of the ESV Bible and as the Theological Editor for the *ESV Study Bible*.

LANE T. DENNIS is President of Crossway, a not-for-profit publishing ministry. Dr. Dennis earned his PhD from Northwestern University. He is Chair of the ESV Bible Translation Oversight Committee and Executive Editor of the *ESV Study Bible*.

DANE C. ORTLUND is Executive Vice President of Bible Publishing and Bible Publisher at Crossway. He is a graduate of Covenant Theological Seminary (MDiv, ThM) and Wheaton College (BA, PhD). Dr. Ortlund has authored several books and scholarly articles in the areas of Bible, theology, and Christian living.

JOEL, AMOS, AND OBADIAH

A 12-WEEK STUDY

Kristofer D. Holroyd

WHEATON, ILLINOIS

Crossway is a publishing ministry of Good News Publishers.

VP			27	26	25	24	23	22	21	20	19	18
15	14	13	12	11	10	9	8	7	6	5	4	3	2	1

TABLE OF CONTENTS

SERIES PREFACE

KNOWING THE BIBLE, as the series title indicates, was created to help readers know and understand the meaning, the message, and the God of the Bible. Each volume in the series consists of 12 units that progressively take the reader through a clear, concise study of one or more books of the Bible. In this way, any given volume can fruitfully be used in a 12-week format either in group study, such as in a church-based context, or in individual study. Of course, these 12 studies could be completed in fewer or more than 12 weeks, as convenient, depending on the context in which they are used.

Each study unit gives an overview of the text at hand before digging into it with a series of questions for reflection or discussion. The unit then concludes by highlighting the gospel of grace in each passage ("Gospel Glimpses"), identifying whole-Bible themes that occur in the passage ("Whole-Bible Connections"), and pinpointing Christian doctrines that are affirmed in the passage ("Theological Soundings").

The final component to each unit is a section for reflecting on personal and practical implications from the passage at hand. The layout provides space for recording responses to the questions proposed, and we think readers need to do this to get the full benefit of the exercise. The series also includes definitions of key words. These definitions are indicated by a note number in the text and are found at the end of each chapter.

Lastly, to help understand the Bible in this deeper way, we urge readers to use the ESV Bible and the *ESV Study Bible*, which are available in various print and digital formats, including online editions at esv.org. The *Knowing the Bible* series is also available online.

May the Lord greatly bless your study as you seek to know him through knowing his Word.

J. I. Packer
Lane T. Dennis

WEEK 1: OVERVIEW

▲

Joel, Amos, and Obadiah were prophets who ministered over a long span of Israel's history, and identifying exactly when each prophet ministered remains difficult, with no real consensus found among Bible scholars. Nevertheless, each of these three prophets anticipates the "day of the Lord." On that day, God will judge the earth and relieve his people from their suffering at the hands of their enemies, refreshing and reestablishing them.

This day of the Lord begins, however, with judgment upon God's own people. God had given Israel his presence, his Word, and a special relationship with him, but they grew complacent and self-indulgent and even took advantage of the weak and impoverished among God's people. Therefore, God promised to begin judgment with his own people, which would arrive through the armies of the Assyrians and the Babylonians.

Even so, God offered hope to his people, if they would but return to him. If his people would turn back to God and away from their false worship, complacency, indulgence, and mistreatment of the weak and impoverished, then God would defeat their enemies, restore them to the Promised Land, and, most importantly, be reconciled to them.

Through our study of the books of Joel, Amos, and Obadiah, which consist primarily of poetry in the form of judgment or vision oracles, we will be confronted with sin and judgment, but we will also be offered the hope of God's salvation through our Savior, Jesus Christ. As the prophets Joel, Amos, and Obadiah awaited a coming day of the Lord, we, too, eagerly await the day of the Lord in which our King and Savior Jesus Christ will return and establish his rule over all nations. (For further background, see the ESV *Study Bible*, pages 1643–1679; available online at www.esv.org.)

Placing These Three Books in the Larger Story

God chose the Israelites out of all the nations of the world to be his witnesses in that world. Their mission was to represent and reveal God by the way they worshiped and lived. Instead, however, throughout her history Israel was no different than the rest of the nations: her wealthy preyed upon the poor, the strong took advantage of the weak, and worship of the Lord devolved into empty rituals. Accordingly, despite the evil in the world around them, judgment would begin with the household of God (1 Pet. 4:17), and God's people would face the fearful day of the Lord. Moreover, if the judgment of God falls first on the people of God, how much more does it fall on his enemies and the enemies of his people! The day of the Lord, then, is a day of judgment for both God's people and the nations of the world. Even so, in the midst of judgment lies salvation, as God promises to establish his rule over the nations, a rule that includes not only Israel but all of God's people gathered from all the nations on earth. This promised salvation anticipates the saving work of Jesus Christ, who would be crowned King of kings and Lord of lords.

Key Verses

"'Yet even now,' declares the LORD, 'return to me with all your heart, with fasting, with weeping, and with mourning; and rend your hearts and not your garments.' Return to the LORD your God, for he is gracious and merciful, slow to anger, and abounding in steadfast love; and he relents over disaster." (Joel 2:12–13)

Date and Historical Background

The Assyrian Empire ruled the ancient Near East[1] for almost a century, but then, around 780–745 BC, the empire waned in power. During this period, both Israel[2] and Judah experienced stability and prosperity. However, Assyria's diminished influence did not last long, and in 745 BC, when Tiglath-pileser III became king of the empire, Assyria once again began to dominate the region. This dominance included the conquering of the northern kingdom of Israel and the relocation of the inhabitants of Israel to other areas throughout Assyria's empire.

Although Judah was spared destruction by the Assyrians, a new world power would soon rise: Babylon. Babylon would supplant Assyria as the predominant empire and in 586 BC would conquer Judah and carry the inhabitants of Judah into exile. Edom,[3] Judah's southeastern neighbor and ethnic cousin, not only refused to help Judah in her times of crisis—especially during the Babylonian assault on Judah—but even took advantage of Judah's various vulnerabilities, plundering Judah whenever possible.

Into these tumultuous times God sent his prophets Joel, Amos, and Obadiah. During their respective ministries, they brought God's perspective on, and explanation for, the surrounding world events.

Outline

Joel

  I. The Judgment against Judah and the Day of the Lord (1:1–2:17)

    A. Locust invasion: Forerunner of the day of the Lord (1:1–20)

    B. Army invasion: The arrival of the day of the Lord (2:1–17)

  II. The Mercy of the Lord and Judgment against the Nations (2:18–3:21)

    A. Mercy: The Lord responds by restoring his people (2:18–32)

    B. Judgment: The Lord's judgment against the nations and his dwelling with his people (3:1–21)

Amos

  I. Superscription (1:1)

  II. Oracles of Judgment (1:2–6:14)

    A. Judgments on Israel's neighbors (1:2–2:5)

    B. Judgments on Israel (2:6–6:14)

      1. Introductory announcement of judgment on Israel (2:6–16)

      2. Detailed announcements of judgment on Israel (3:1–6:14)

        a. An oracle of warning (3:1–15)

        b. An oracle of doom (4:1–13)

        c. An oracle of entreaty (5:1–17)

        d. An oracle of woe (5:18–6:14)

III. Visions of Judgment (7:1–9:15)

    A. A vision of inescapable judgment (7:1–17)

        1. The vision itself (7:1–9)
        2. An experience reinforcing the vision (7:10–17)

    B. A vision of the terrible end (8:1–14)

    C. A vision of the Lord standing beside the altar (9:1–15)

        1. The thresholds shaken (9:1–10)
        2. The booth of David restored (9:11–15)

Obadiah

    I. First Announcement of Judgment to Edom (vv. 1–4)

    II. Second Announcement of Judgment to Edom (vv. 5–7)

    III. Announcement of Judgment, Accusation, and Warning to Edom (vv. 8–15)

    IV. Promise of Restoration and Victory to Israel (vv. 16–18)

    V. Promise of Restoration and Yahweh's Kingship (vv. 19–21)

As You Get Started

Read through each book—Joel, Amos, and Obadiah—straight through in one sitting. What are your first impressions? What stands out to you?

What words, phrases, and themes seem to span across these three books?

What questions do you have as you begin this study?

> ## As You Finish This Unit . . .

Take a few minutes to ask God to bless you with increased understanding and a transformed heart and life as you begin this study of Joel, Amos, and Obadiah.

Definitions

[1] **Ancient Near East** – The land, people, and cultures of early civilizations in the region roughly corresponding to the modern Middle East.

[2] **Israel** – Originally, another name given to Jacob (Gen. 32:28). Later applied to the nation formed by his descendants, then to the 10 northern tribes of that nation, who rejected the anointed king and formed their own nation. In the NT, the name is applied to the church as the spiritual descendants of Abraham (Gal. 6:16).

[3] **Edom** – The nation established by the descendants of Esau (see Genesis 25–28); throughout history, the fraternal strife between Jacob and Esau continued to show itself in the strife between Israel and Edom.

WEEK 2: LOCUSTS AND ARMIES

Chapter 1

Themes, words, phrases
− destruction
− desolation
− lacking
− sadness
− call to mourn
− parched

Joel 1:1–2:17

> ## The Place of the Passage

The book of Joel opens with a description of the aftermath of a terrible locust plague. The prophet Joel, in light of the devastation left by the plague, calls God's people to grieve and lament the destruction. This destruction and lamentation provide the occasion for Joel to warn of an invading army that will come from the north and, like the locusts, will bring about devastation to the land and people. Joel's warning of the invading army is a call to Judah to repent and turn back to the Lord, who is gracious and merciful and may relent of the impending judgment.

> ## The Big Picture

God is bringing judgment on Judah; however, it is not too late to repent, turn back to God, and receive his mercy.

Lament → a passionate expression of grief

13

> ## Reflection and Discussion

Read through the complete passage for this study, Joel 1:1–2:17. Then write your reflections on the following questions. (For further background, see the *ESV Study Bible*, pages 1646–1650; available online at www.esv.org.)

1. Locust Invasion (1:1–1:20) *Forerunner in the day of the Lord*

The locust, a kin of the grasshopper, can travel in large swarms and bring devastation upon all surrounding plant life. Describe the devastation that the locust plague has brought upon Judah, as recorded by Joel.

It came in 3 waves of devastation.

V.12 gladness dries up from the children of man

To lament "like a virgin . . . for the bridegroom of her youth" would be to experience grief like that of an engaged woman whose fiancé dies before the marriage. Read verses 8–12 again. Try to imagine what it must have been like for the people living in the aftermath of this terrible plague. How does Joel depict the people's suffering?

no hope

Such heartbreak for her fiance

Have you ever experienced such total devastation either personally or as part of a community or nation? What was it like for you to endure such devastation?

Read verses 13–20 again. How does Joel tell the people to respond to their grief?

Joel 1:15 reminds the readers that destruction comes from God Almighty. How does it feel to be confronted with the truth that the Lord himself brought this devastation upon his own people?

----

2. Army Invasion (2:1–2:17)

Review the possible interpretations of the locust invasion given in the *ESV Study Bible*, page 1644. It seems that God is using the past experience of a locust plague to describe the future invasion of a foreign nation's army. Read through Joel 2:1–11 and note below the ways in which the army is compared to a locust plague.

Joel does not provide a reason for this predicted invasion; however, the people of Israel should already know why such an invasion might happen. Earlier in Israel's history, God had given them their land, the land of Canaan, where they were to live in relationship with him and to reveal and represent him to the nations of the world. As the people prepared to enter into that land, God made certain promises to his people (Deuteronomy 28), promises that included blessings for obedience and curses for disobedience. The curses included such things as the locusts consuming their fields (Deut. 28:38), the crickets possessing their trees and fruit (Deut. 28:42), and the people's being oppressed by a foreign nation (Deut. 28:36). Read Deuteronomy 28:45–51. Why might this foreign army described in the book of Joel be invading Judah?

In light of Deuteronomy 28:47, why does Joel tell the people to rend their hearts and not their garments[1] (Joel 2:12–13)? What does it mean to "rend" their hearts?

In what areas of your life are you not serving the Lord your God "with joyfulness and gladness of heart"? What would it look like for you to "rend your hearts and not your garments" and to "return to [the Lord] with all your heart"?

Read through the following three sections on *Gospel Glimpses, Whole-Bible Connections,* and *Theological Soundings.* Then take time to consider the *Personal Implications* these sections may have for you.

Gospel Glimpses

JUDGMENT FOR SIN. God's holiness[2] and perfect character demand that same perfect morality from all people. When we fail to obey God's demands, that disobedience—sin—earns God's judgment. Just as a violation of civil law earns the penalties of the law, so do violations of God's character and laws earn his judgment and penalties. Sometimes, as in the case for Israel during the ministry of the prophet Joel, such judgment comes in this life, with tangible consequences for sin, such as locust plagues or invading armies. On the other hand, it sometimes seems that the disobedient do not suffer judgment in this life. Nevertheless, through consequences in this life or in the life to come, God always judges sin, and all people will one day stand before him and receive from him according to what they have done, "whether good or evil" (2 Cor. 5:10).

REPENTANCE. Repentance is a change of heart and mind over one's attitude toward God or one's actions; it is a turning away from sin and a turning toward God. Accordingly, repentance involves more than just an external confession of guilt or expression of regret; rather, this inward change of heart and mind must result in a grieving over the wrong committed, a hating of the offense, and an earnest desire for the mercy and forgiveness of God. Such repentance necessarily results in changed behavior. See Jeremiah 31:18–19 and 2 Corinthians 7:10–11.

Whole-Bible Connections

LAMENTING. Throughout the Bible we see whole groups of people weeping over disaster, such as the nation of Israel weeping over the near extinction of the tribe of Benjamin in Judges 21. We see families weep in times of hardship, such as Naomi and her daughters-in-law in Ruth 1. And we see individuals weep in sorrow, such as Abraham at the death of his wife in Genesis 23. Moreover, an entire book of the Bible (Lamentations) is dedicated to mourning the destruction of Jerusalem, and even our Lord Jesus Christ wept at the death of his friend Lazarus (John 11) and over his people's rejecting him (Matthew 23:37–39; Luke 19:41–44). Grieving, weeping, and lamenting are part of experiencing life in this world, but God's people do not grieve like the rest of the world. For example, the resurrection of Jesus Christ teaches us to grieve with hope in the future (1 Thess. 4:13–14), and godly sorrow leads us to examine ourselves and turn from sin in repentance to God through faith[3] in Jesus Christ (2 Cor. 7:9–10).

THE DAY OF THE LORD. The "day of the Lord" is a frequent theme in the books of the prophets. It variously heralds a day in which God judges unfaithfulness among his people; a day in which God comes to judge the nations; and/or a day in which God establishes his throne and rules over the nations, saving his people. In the New Testament, this same theme is taken up to describe the return of Christ Jesus. For more on the day of the Lord, see the *ESV Study Bible*, pages 1668–1669.

Theological Soundings

SOVEREIGN DISASTERS. Israel as a nation had a special relationship with God, unlike any nation today. Because of this special relationship, there existed in her day a much closer connection between national hardships, such as natural disasters, and the sin of God's people. Nevertheless, the Lord God Almighty rules over all things, all places, and all people. Nothing happens outside of or apart from his will, his plans, and his purposes. This means that, even today, disasters happen underneath God's sovereign will: either he *allows* them or he directly *causes* them. Although God sometimes allows bad things to happen (for example, read the book of Job and see how God allows the Enemy to bring about harm), he sometimes brings disaster himself. Such disasters may be a punishment for sin or may function for some other purpose within God's plans and purposes. Regardless of why they happen, such disasters point us to the coming judgment of God, when all people will be required to give an account not only for their deeds (Rev. 22:12) but even for their very words (Matt. 12:36–37).

PROMISED LAND. God promised Abraham that his descendants would inhabit the land of Canaan, and eventually they did. After the exodus from Egypt and the wandering in the wilderness because of their disobedience, the Israelites finally entered into the Promised Land, taking possession of it and establishing what would eventually be the kingdom of Israel. However, because of Israel's constant rebellion against God, which included worshiping idols, seeking alliances with neighboring nations instead of trusting in God's protection, and abusing the weak and impoverished among them, God eventually took the Israelites out of the Promised Land. Israel would later return to the land, after the defeat of Babylon; however, the kingdom of Israel would never really be fully established again as an autonomous kingdom. Instead, with the coming of Jesus Christ, God's people look to a new, spiritual Promised Land, a new Jerusalem that Christ will establish and from which he will rule when he returns (Revelation 21).

Personal Implications

Take time to reflect on the implications of Joel 1:1–2:17 for your own life today. Consider what you have learned that might lead you to praise God, repent of sin, and trust in his gracious promises. Write down your reflections under the three headings we have considered and on the passage as a whole.

1. Gospel Glimpses

2. Whole-Bible Connections

3. Theological Soundings

4. Joel 1:1–2:17

> ## As You Finish This Unit . . .

Take a moment now to ask for the Lord's blessing and help as you continue in this study of Joel, Amos, and Obadiah. And take a moment also to look back through this unit of study, to reflect on some key things that the Lord may be teaching you.

Definitions

[1] **Rending garments** – Tearing one's clothes was an ancient expression of intense grief and sorrow.

[2] **Holiness** – A quality possessed by something or someone set apart for special use. When applied to God, it refers to his utter perfection and complete transcendence over creation. God's people are called to imitate his holiness (Lev. 19:2), which means being set apart from sin and reserved for his purposes.

[3] **Faith** – Trust in or reliance upon something or someone despite a lack of concrete proof. Salvation, which is purely a work of God's grace, can be received only through faith (Rom. 5:2; Eph. 2:8–9). The writer of Hebrews calls on believers to emulate those who lived godly lives by faith (Hebrews 11).

WEEK 3: THE LORD HAD PITY ON HIS PEOPLE

Joel 2:18–32

The Place of the Passage

Because of God's love for his people and even for creation itself, he promises to restore and refresh his people by defeating and removing the invading army. In the wake of this deliverance, God will again bless the people and the land, restoring to them what they have lost. The primary blessings, though, will be reconciliation with God, removal of their shame, and the coming of the Holy Spirit[1] upon all who call on the name of the Lord.

The Big Picture

This passage anticipates the coming salvation in which God will defeat the enemies of his people and pour out his Spirit into their hearts.

Reflection and Discussion

Read through the complete passage for this study, Joel 2:18–32. Then write your reflections on the following questions. (For further background, see the *ESV Study Bible*, pages 1650–1652; available online at www.esv.org.)

1. The Lord's Pity (2:18–27)

Joel 2:18 explains the reason for God's mercy upon Judah: he "became jealous for his land." What does it mean for God to be jealous for his land?

Verses 21–22 instruct the land and beasts not to be afraid but instead to rejoice. Read Romans 8:19–22. Why would the land and beasts be afraid?

From Joel 2:18–22 and Romans 8:19–22, what is the effect of God's salvation of his people upon the land and the rest of creation?

Review your answers from week 2, section 1: "Locust Invasion." Then reread Joel 2:24–25. What are these verses promising? What hope is being offered?

In your own life, what are your "years that the swarming locust has eaten"? What restoration are you longing for?

Simple restoration of lifestyle or material goods is not the primary goal of God's mercy to his people. Read verses 26–27. What is the ultimate goal of God's mercy?

2. The Lord's Spirit (2:28–32)

The salvation of God's people culminates in his presence among them (v. 27). Read verses 28–29 and note the different people groups upon which God will pour out his Spirit.

The pouring out of the Holy Spirit comes upon all of God's people without regard to race, gender, or socioeconomic status (see also Gal. 3:26–29). How might this truth impact our relationships with others?

In light of what we have already seen regarding the salvation of God's people and the impact this salvation has on the rest of creation, why do you think such wonders in creation occur alongside the "day of the Lord" and the outpouring of the Holy Spirit (Joel 2:30–31)? What do these wonders have to do with calling on the name of the Lord (v. 32)?

Read Romans 10:8–13. What does it mean to "call on the name of the Lord"?

What is the relationship between being called by the Lord at the end of verse 32 and calling on the Lord at the beginning of the verse?

Read through the following three sections on *Gospel Glimpses*, *Whole-Bible Connections*, and *Theological Soundings*. Then take time to consider the *Personal Implications* these sections may have for you.

Gospel Glimpses

A JEALOUS GOD. Jealousy or envy in the sense of wanting something that we do not have and that belongs to others is, of course, condemned by Scripture (e.g., Ex. 20:17 and Gal. 5:20–21). However, to be jealous for something that belongs exclusively to us is a godly form of jealousy, especially when that which belongs to us is being threatened by another. A husband shows godly jealousy when another man makes advances toward his wife (Prov. 6:32–35). The apostle Paul shows godly jealousy when false teachers threaten to lead the church astray (2 Cor. 11:1–6). It is in this sense that God is jealous for his people and for the land he gave them. When God's people give to false gods the worship that belongs to the Lord alone, he is jealous (Ex. 20:4–6), and when foreign armies invade the land God gave to his people, he is jealous (Joel 2:18; Zech. 1:14–17).

THE CROSS OF SHAME. Our sin not only results in our guilt before God; it also brings with it the feelings of shame associated with that guilt. In the Old Testament, the consequences of sin often include losing in battle, suffering plagues or droughts, and eventually even becoming slaves of other nations. Such consequences result in becoming the object of scorn of those other nations, who would mock and taunt the victims of such devastations. The shame felt by Israel in such situations gives us an image of the spiritual shame we experience from our sin, which alienates us from God. But for our sake, Jesus "endured the cross, despising the shame" (Heb. 12:2), feeling fully its scorn, mockery, and alienation. Crucifixion was particularly shameful for a circumcised[2] Jewish man in a Gentile culture, because typically those crucified would be hung on the cross naked.

Whole-Bible Connections

THE PRESENCE OF GOD. The presence of God with his people was visibly demonstrated to Israel through a cloud and fire. For example, when God led his people out of Egypt, he led them with fire at night and a cloud during the day (Ex. 13:17–22); when God met with Moses on Mount Sinai, the Lord's presence was demonstrated visibly by fire and smoke (Ex. 19:16–20); and once the Tent of Meeting (and later, the temple) was built, God's presence among his people was shown by cloud and fire (Ex. 40:34–38; 1 Kings 8:10–11). But a day was coming, Joel promised, when the presence of God would dwell within his people (Joel 2:28–32). Indeed, after the resurrection and ascension[3] of Jesus Christ, the Holy Spirit came upon all God's people (Acts 2; see especially vv. 17–21, which quote Joel 2:28–32), and we, the people of God, have become the new temple of the Lord's presence (1 Cor. 6:19–20).

CREATION GROANING. When Adam and Eve disobeyed God in the garden of Eden, one of the effects of their sin was the cursing of creation. Because of the sin of our first parents, thorns and thistles infest the ground and work becomes laborious and difficult (see Gen. 3:17–19 and the note on those verses in the *ESV Study Bible*, page 56). Additionally, creation constantly suffers from the sin of humankind: our overuse, misuse, and abuse of God's good creation. For this reason, creation eagerly awaits the return of Jesus Christ and the removal of sin and its effects from the world (Rom. 8:19–25).

Theological Soundings

THE UNIVERSAL OFFER OF SALVATION. Perhaps the best-known verse in the Bible, John 3:16, promises that "whoever believes" in Jesus will have eternal life, and in our passage this week, Joel promises salvation to "everyone who calls on the name of the LORD." The good news of the gospel, the free gift of salvation, is to be offered to everyone. Accordingly, Jesus sends out his disciples by telling them to make disciples of "all nations" (Matt. 28:19); Paul notes that God "commands all people everywhere to repent" (Acts 17:30–31), and the Bible ends with an invitation to everyone who thirsts to come to the water of life (Rev. 22:17). Furthermore, each of these passages pertains to God's people inviting others to "the water of life." Just as Jesus sent out his disciples, so he sends us out to offer to all people this glorious salvation in the name of the Lord (see 2 Cor. 5:11–21).

THE PARTICULAR RESPONSE FOR SALVATION. Even though the offer of salvation is to be given to everyone, not everyone will respond to it. Our sins have so corrupted us that the apostle Paul refers to us as "dead" in our sins (Eph. 2:1). What can a dead person do? Nothing! Not even respond to the offer of salvation. Therefore, God must first make us alive in Christ (Eph. 2:4–5) so that we can turn to him, believe, and be saved (see John 3:5–8). Accordingly, as Joel notes in our passage this week, "Everyone who calls on the name of the LORD shall be saved," but those who will indeed call, those who escape and are saved, are only "those whom the Lord calls" (Joel 2:32). In other words, only those whom the Lord makes alive and enables to call on the name of the Lord will indeed be saved.

Personal Implications

Take time to reflect on the implications of Joel 2:18–32 for your own life today. Consider what you have learned that might lead you to praise God, repent of sin, and trust in his gracious promises. Write down your reflections under the three headings we have considered and on the passage as a whole.

1. Gospel Glimpses

2. Whole-Bible Connections

3. Theological Soundings

4. Joel 2:18–32

> **As You Finish This Unit . . .**

Take a moment now to ask for the Lord's blessing and help as you continue in this study of Joel, Amos, and Obadiah. And take a moment also to look back through this unit of study, to reflect on some key things that the Lord may be teaching you.

Definitions

[1] **Holy Spirit** – One of the persons of the Trinity, and thus fully God. The Bible mentions several roles of the Holy Spirit, including convicting people of sin, bringing them to conversion, indwelling them, empowering them to live in righteousness and faithfulness, supporting them in times of trial, and enabling them to understand the Scriptures. The Holy Spirit inspired the writers of Scripture, guiding them to record the very words of God. The Holy Spirit was especially active in Jesus' life and ministry on earth (e.g., Luke 3:22).

[2] **Circumcision** – The ritual practice of removing the foreskin of an individual, which was commanded for all male Israelites in OT times as a sign of participation in the covenant God established with Abraham (Gen. 17:9–14).

[3] **Ascension** – The departure of the resurrected Jesus to God the Father in heaven (Luke 24:50–51; Acts 1:1–12).

WEEK 4: THE LORD DWELLS IN ZION

Joel 3:1–21

The Place of the Passage

After God uses the locust plague of chapter 1 to warn of an invading army of judgment from the north, in chapter 2, his people repent and turn back to him, and the Lord takes pity on them. Now, in light of their restored relationship with God, his people await his judgment upon their enemies. In due time, God takes his seat as judge of the nations and holds court against them, charging them with their crimes and pronouncing the guilty verdict and impending punishment. This judgment of God and vindication of his people promises full restoration of God's people, and the book of Joel closes with hope, "for the LORD dwells in Zion."[1]

The Big Picture

Although God's judgment against his enemies and the enemies of his people seems delayed, God's justice will prevail and his people will be vindicated; until that day, his people hide in him, for he is their refuge and stronghold.

Reflection and Discussion

Read through the complete passage for this study, Joel 3:1–21. Then write your reflections on the following questions. (For further background, see the *ESV Study Bible*, pages 1652–1654; available online at www.esv.org.)

1. A Lawsuit (3:1–8)

The Lord Almighty is Judge of the earth, and the Bible often presents his judgments in the form of a lawsuit (e.g., Psalm 82; Isa. 41:21–29; Jer. 2:5–13; Micah 6). Joel 3:1–8 similarly brings charges and a verdict against Tyre, Sidon, and Philistia. Read the passage again and list the charges.

In verses 5 and 6, the Lord takes personally the attack against his people. The plundering of the temple is a taking of "my" silver and "my" gold and "my" treasures. What is the significance of God's response being expressed in this manner?

In this lawsuit against God's enemies, what is the verdict and the punishment?

The law of retaliation, sometimes called *lex talionis*, is a matching of the punishment to fit the crime. How does the punishment against Tyre, Sidon, and Philistia exemplify this law of retaliation—that is, how does the punishment fit the crime?

How does the fact that God still repays his enemies and the enemies of his people according to the law of retaliation affect your desire for justice now and in the future?

2. Judgment on God's Enemies (3:9–16)

These verses describe the desperate situation of the enemy of God. Read the verses again and note some of the extreme pictures of the enemy's desperation.

Generations before Israel entered the Promised Land, God promised Abraham that his descendants would take possession of the land, but not until the sin of the people in the land was "complete" (Gen. 15:16). Here in Joel, the prophet notes that the sin of God's enemies is now full and overflowing (Joel 3:13). The

Bible often depicts God's people as being in a time of waiting for the judgment of God against his and our enemies, a time of waiting for deliverance and salvation. Read Psalm 13. In what ways are God's people waiting for deliverance today?

Read Joel 3:16 again. What does it mean that God is a refuge and a stronghold to his people?

3. The Lord Dwells in Zion (3:17–21)

Just as the Lord repays his enemies according to the law of retaliation, he also restores the blessings of his people according to what they have lost. How does this passage reverse the effects of the locust plague and invading army from Joel 1–2?

Joel ends with the promise that "the Lord dwells in Zion." How is the eternal presence of God in the midst of his people an assurance in times of suffering?

What is the ultimate goal of enduring God's suffering, while awaiting his judgment upon his enemies and the eventual salvation of his people (3:17)?

Where in your life is God revealing himself to you? What situations are you enduring through which God is drawing you to himself? Where is he calling you to "know that I am the LORD your God"?

Read through the following three sections on *Gospel Glimpses*, *Whole-Bible Connections*, and *Theological Soundings*. Then take time to consider the *Personal Implications* these sections may have for you.

Gospel Glimpses

THE LEAST OF THESE. The judgment in this week's passage against those who mistreat the young boys and girls of Israel (Joel 3:3) echoes God's love of the orphan, the widow, and the weak, as seen throughout Scripture (e.g., James 1:27). Similar to the depiction of God in this passage in Joel, Jesus in Matthew 25:31–46 sits on the throne in judgment against those who have neglected people who are hungry, thirsty, strangers, naked, sick, or in prison. Conversely, he welcomes and rewards those who feed the hungry, give drink to the thirsty, welcome the stranger, clothe the naked, and visit the sick and the prisoner. Love of God means love for those he loves, especially the weak and downtrodden of the world.

KNOW THE LORD. God's actions in history for the salvation of his people are ultimately so that we may know that he alone is God and that he alone saves humanity. To "know the Lord," then, is to know that God is the one who made all things out of nothing, to know that God alone stands as sovereign ruler and judge over all people, and to know that God alone can save us from sin, death, darkness, and all of his and our enemies. For this reason, the Lord says, "Be still, and know that I am God" (Ps. 46:10).

▶ Whole-Bible Connections

PLOWSHARES AND SWORDS. Isaiah 2:1–4 and Micah 4:1–4 promise that, at the end of time, there will be such peace for God's people that the nations will no longer need their military arsenals. Through the picture of turning swords and spears into farming tools, the prophets herald a lasting peace for God's people, a peace that no longer knows the art of war. On the other hand, that coming day of the Lord promises judgment and war for the enemies of God. In a reversal of the picture from Isaiah and Micah, our passage this week images the devastation and hopelessness on that day for the Lord's enemies; their desperation is shown through the turning of farming tools into battle instruments and a call to arms such that even the weak must stand and fight.

LIVING WATER. The Bible often describes our spiritual longings in terms of thirst. For example, Psalm 42 describes our soul's longing for God in terms of a deer's thirst for water, and Isaiah 55 invites all who thirst to come to the waters so that "your soul may live" (Isa. 55:3). This same invitation closes the Bible in Revelation 22:17. In fact, just as the first book of the Bible describes the garden of Eden in terms of the rivers that flow in and through it (Gen. 2:10–14), so the book of Revelation describes our future life with God with a picture of the river of life that runs through the new city of God (Rev. 22:1–5). Accordingly, Jesus says, "Blessed are those who hunger and thirst for righteousness,[2] for they shall be satisfied" (Matt. 5:6).

▶ Theological Soundings

VINDICATION. God's people all over the world and all throughout history have suffered persecution for the sake of the gospel. Indeed, Jesus promises such persecution: the world will hate us because the world hates him (John 15:18–25). The Lord does promise deliverance and even vengeance upon his enemies and the enemies of his people, but that vindication can sometimes feel slow in coming. Indeed, we may not ever see such vindication in this life (see Rev. 6:9–11). Nevertheless, the Bible promises that such deliverance and vindication will indeed come in the Lord's perfect timing. And on that last day, God's people will be vindicated and his justice against his enemies will be executed.

WHOSE REVENGE? When we suffer hurt and harm from others, we can be tempted toward revenge: *lex talionis*, or "an eye for an eye." In the Old Testament, retaliation laws were given to the civil authorities, not to individuals, in order to provide appropriate justice and eliminate evil. Furthermore, such laws even guarded against excessive or inappropriate punishment, thereby protecting the perpetrators. Such justice points to the pure and perfect justice of God: "'Vengeance is mine, I will repay,' says the Lord" (Rom. 12:19; compare Deut. 32:35). Accordingly, God's perfect justice enables us to forgive those who hurt or harm us, because we know that God himself will make all things right—which will include punishing the wicked.

Personal Implications

Take time to reflect on the implications of Joel 3:1–21 for your own life today. Consider what you have learned that might lead you to praise God, repent of sin, and trust in his gracious promises. Write down your reflections under the three headings we have considered and on the passage as a whole.

1. Gospel Glimpses

2. Whole-Bible Connections

3. Theological Soundings

4. Joel 3:1–21

As You Finish This Unit . . .

Take a moment now to ask for the Lord's blessing and help as you continue in this study of Joel, Amos, and Obadiah. And take a moment also to look back through this unit of study, to reflect on some key things that the Lord may be teaching you.

Definitions

[1] **Zion** – A synonym for Jerusalem, sometimes used to refer to a specific hill or mountain in Jerusalem (Mount Zion).

[2] **Righteousness** – The quality of being morally right and without sin. One of God's distinctive attributes. God imputes righteousness to (justifies) those who trust in Jesus Christ. "Unrighteousness" describes the absence of righteousness, or behavior contrary to or absent of righteousness.

WEEK 5: A SETUP

Amos 1:1–2:5

▲

The Place of the Passage

The book of Amos begins with prophetic words of judgment against the nations surrounding Israel, the northern kingdom of the Israelite people. These opening verses also include judgments against the southern Israelite kingdom, Judah. These judgments condemn the nations for their treatment of Israel and even for their treatment of each other, revealing that all must give an account before God for their actions. This section turns in chapter 2 to a judgment against Judah, who is held to a higher standard because of her knowledge of God's law.[1] Throughout this beginning section, we can easily imagine the people of Israel (the northern kingdom) nodding in smug agreement over the judgment against their neighbors and their southern rival, Judah. But Amos is subtly setting them up to hear their own judgment in the following chapters.

The Big Picture

God reigns sovereignly over all things, all places, and all people, and all must give an account to him for their actions.

> ### Reflection and Discussion

Read through the complete passage for this study, Amos 1:1–2:5. Then write your reflections on the following questions. (For further background, see the *ESV Study Bible*, pages 1659–1661; available online at www.esv.org.)

1. Judgment on the Nations (1:1–2:3)

The book of Amos opens with judgment oracles[2] against the nations surrounding Israel. Use the map in the *ESV Study Bible*, page 1657, to locate the cities of Damascus, Gaza, and Tyre, and the nations of Edom, Ammon, Moab, and Judah. What strikes you about the location of these recipients of God's judgment?

Although these oracles condemn nations for their treatment of other nations and peoples, the moral principles upon which they are judged easily translate to us today. Consider the following specific judgments and reflect on your own life and temptation toward similar practices.

Damascus. The sin of Damascus seems to be its trampling upon the people of Gilead, treating them as nothing more than a pile of grain (see the note on verse 3 in the *ESV Study Bible*, page 1659). How have you treated people as less than human? How have you trampled upon others?

Tyre. The sin of Tyre includes their failure to keep their word; they did not keep the promises they made to the nation of Edom. How have you failed to keep your word, your commitments, or your obligations? What promises have you broken?

Edom. Note the end of 1:11. Edom is judged for the nation's perpetual anger. How does anger manifest itself in your life? Where are you slow to forgive? How are you holding onto hurts against you? How are you growing bitterness in your heart?

_____

_____

_____

_____

Ammon. The nation of Ammon was so violent and vicious that they even "ripped open pregnant women." How has violence taken root in your heart? Where do you revel in it? How has the violence in the world around you, in the media, or in entertainment developed a love of violence in you?

_____

_____

_____

_____

In each of the judgments against foreign nations thus far, the crimes have included actions against Israel, attacks in some form against God's people. In the judgment against Moab, however, the nation is condemned because of its actions against Edom, a neighbor to Israel. Read Romans 1:18–22. Why do these oracles of judgment include judgment against a nation that does not know God and that does not seem to be harming God's people?

_____

_____

_____

_____

2. Judgment on Judah (2:4–5)

Why is Judah judged? What crime has Judah committed?

_____

_____

_____

_____

What are the lies that have led Judah astray?

Read Hebrews 10:26–28. How is judgment against Judah different from judgment against the other nations named so far in Amos?

Read through the following three sections on *Gospel Glimpses*, *Whole-Bible Connections*, and *Theological Soundings*. Then take time to consider the *Personal Implications* these sections may have for you.

Gospel Glimpses

NO EXCUSES. God's existence, his attributes, and his power are all clearly seen in creation. Justice, mercy, and how to treat other people are evident to everyone. This general knowledge of God renders all humankind accountable to him, as Paul notes in Romans 1:18–23. All people are accountable for how they live and for whether or not they live for God's honor and in thankfulness to him for all he has given. Accordingly, all who continually fail to acknowledge and honor God will face his wrath and judgment.

A HIGHER STANDARD. Those who have heard the Word of God, that is, his law and his good news of the gospel of Jesus Christ, are held to an even higher standard of accountability. Not only do they have the general knowledge of God from creation; they also have benefited by hearing directly from him through his Word about who he is and what he requires of humanity. Therefore, those who hear the Word of God and reject it are in danger of even greater judgment.

Whole-Bible Connections

ORACLES AGAINST THE NATIONS. Throughout the Old Testament, God's prophets deliver messages not just to his people but also to the nations of the world at that time. This includes, for example, Jonah's message to Nineveh, through which the inhabitants of Nineveh learn of God's mercy and forgiveness (see the book of Jonah). Most often, however, these messages are pronouncements of judgment in which God demonstrates that he rules not just over his people but over all the nations of the world. See the chart in the *ESV Study Bible*, page 1264, for an overview of the oracles against the nations throughout the prophetic books.

PROMISE KEEPER. God does not and cannot lie, because such dishonesty would violate his very character (Heb. 6:18). Furthermore, God's Word is truth (John 17:17), which means not just that God's Word is true but that when he speaks, that word is truth itself: the embodiment and standard of truth against which every other word is to be tested. Accordingly, when God speaks, his word can be trusted and relied upon. Moreover, since God's word is truth, he expects men and women to speak truth: not just to keep oaths, vows, contracts, or promises but also to speak in such a way that their word is reliable and trustworthy (Matt. 5:33–37).

Theological Soundings

THE SOVEREIGN LORD. The pronouncements of judgment over the nations throughout the Bible remind us of God's sovereign rule. He alone has all power and authority, and he alone is truly immortal (1 Tim. 6:15–16). With such absolute power and authority, he rules over all things, all places, and all people. No one and nothing are outside of his control, and he alone is the God who establishes nations and tears them down (see Jer. 1:10).

HUMAN DIGNITY. Humans are made in the image of God (Gen. 1:27); therefore, an attack on a fellow human is an attack on God himself. Genesis 9:6 makes this clear when God warns Noah, "Whoever sheds the blood of man, by man shall his blood be shed, for God made man in his own image." Moreover, this dignity of humanity impacts even how we speak to and about one another (James 3:9–10). Consequently, all human life is valuable and should be treated with respect and dignity, regardless of age, race, ethnicity, socioeconomic status, physical or emotional ability, or any other characteristic by which we distinguish between people.

> ### Personal Implications

Take time to reflect on the implications of Amos 1:1–2:5 for your own life today. Consider what you have learned that might lead you to praise God, repent of sin, and trust in his gracious promises. Write down your reflections under the three headings we have considered and on the passage as a whole.

1. Gospel Glimpses

2. Whole-Bible Connections

3. Theological Soundings

4. Amos 1:1–2:5

Take a moment now to ask for the Lord's blessing and help as you continue in this study of Joel, Amos, and Obadiah. And take a moment also to look back through this unit of study, to reflect on some key things that the Lord may be teaching you.

Definitions

[1] **Law** – When spelled with an initial capital letter, "Law" refers to the first five books of the Bible. The Law contains numerous commands of God to his people, including the Ten Commandments and instructions regarding worship, sacrifice, and life in Israel. The NT often uses "the law" (lower case) to refer to the entire body of precepts set forth in the books of the Law.

[2] **Oracle** – From Latin "to speak." In the Bible, this term refers to a divine pronouncement delivered through a human agent.

WEEK 6: THE LORD HAS DONE IT

Amos 2:6–3:15

▲

The Place of the Passage

After announcing judgment on the nations surrounding Israel—including even Judah—Amos suddenly turns and, likely to the surprise and even shock of the Israelites, announces judgment upon Israel, too. God had chosen Israel out of all the families on the earth, delivered them from Egypt, defeated their enemies, and brought them into the Promised Land. Nevertheless, Israel turned away from the Lord, even rejecting the prophets and profaning the Nazirites.[1] Therefore, the Lord of Hosts, the God who brings disaster, will bring judgment upon Israel.

The Big Picture

God's own people, who trample upon his grace,[2] will not escape judgment; even so, the Lord reveals his ways through his Word so that his people will turn back to him.

> ### Reflection and Discussion

Read through the complete passage for this study, Amos 2:6–3:15. Then write your reflections on the following questions. (For further background, see the *ESV Study Bible*, pages 1661–1664; available online at www.esv.org.)

1. Judgment on Israel (2:6–16)

As the Israelites hear the judgments Amos proclaims against their neighboring nations, we can easily imagine the growing enthusiasm over the destruction of their enemies. With each new "For three transgressions[3] . . . and for four," anticipation would grow as the Israelites eagerly awaited whichever people group might be named next. But then Amos names Israel itself (v. 6). How might this anticipation and then this sudden turn impact how the judgment against Israel would be received by the Israelites?

What are the sins of Israel listed in these verses?

The Amorites, mentioned in verses 9 and 10, represent the people living in the Promised Land when God gave the land to the Israelites. How does God's salvation of Israel from Egypt, his fighting for the Israelites, and his gift of the Promised Land add weight to this judgment against Israel?

As a follower of Jesus, who has saved us from sin and death, has fought against the powers of darkness on our behalf, and has given us eternal life, how are you challenged by these verses?

---

2. The Lord Has Done It (3:1–15)

In 3:1, what is the relationship between God's choosing of Israel ("You only have I known") and his judgment of Israel ("therefore I will punish you")?

Read verses 3–6 again. The ESV Study Bible notes that, when facing disaster, "the people should not attribute it to bad luck but should take note that God is at work" (page 1663, note on 3:3–8). What impact should it have on us to see even disaster as God's work?

Amos says, "The Lord GOD does nothing without revealing his secret to his servants the prophets" (v. 7; see also Joel 3:17). What does this mean? Why does God reveal his secret to the prophets?

Read 3:12–15 again. Why is disaster coming upon Israel?

Read through the following three sections on *Gospel Glimpses*, *Whole-Bible Connections*, and *Theological Soundings*. Then take time to consider the *Personal Implications* these sections may have for you.

▶ Gospel Glimpses

MANIPULATING GOD. The nations surrounding Israel worshiped fertility gods, false gods that they believed ruled over the fertility of the land, their crops, and their families. These nations would often engage in ritual prostitution, believing that if they practiced physical intimacy with the temple prostitutes, the gods would engage in physical intimacy with each other and thereby make the land, their crops, and their families fertile and productive. This prostitution was an attempt to manipulate the gods into doing or giving them what they wanted. The Israelites, likewise, often fell into practicing such false forms of worship (see 2:7 and the corresponding notes in the *ESV Study Bible*). Instead of responding to the gifts of God's grace, such as salvation from Egypt and entrance into the Promised Land, the Israelites practiced false worship by attempting to manipulate God into giving them the things they wanted so that they could spend what they received on their own pleasures (compare James 4:1–4). We, too, are easily tempted to the false worship of manipulation when we try to earn or buy God's favor solely out of a motivation to make our lives easier and better, instead of pursuing lives motivated by thankful hearts that long to give praise and honor to God for his grace and salvation.

REVEALING HIS SECRETS. Instead of leaving his people to guess as to why bad things happen in this life, particularly to his people in the Old Testament, God reveals the secret that he, himself, has done it (Amos 3:6). This revelation is an act of kindness and love to his people, both then and now, because it draws us to know him better. His power over nations leads us to marvel at his awesome power; his judgment calls us to repentance; his mercy drives us to worship.

▶ Whole-Bible Connections

LORD OF HOSTS. God's almighty power is sometimes demonstrated through the image of a commander leading the armies, or "hosts," of heaven ("the Lord GOD, the God of hosts"; Amos 3:13). For example, the Lord of hosts shows Elisha's servant the armies of the Lord encamped around them (2 Kings 6:17), and Jesus notes that his Father in heaven would send "more than twelve legions of angels" to fight for him if he but asked (Matt. 26:53). This title of God reminds us that he fights for his people (Deut. 1:30–31), and it anticipates the return of the King of kings and Lord of lords with the armies of heaven to establish his kingdom fully and finally (Rev. 19:11–16). (Various forms of the phrase "LORD of hosts" occur nearly 300 times in the Old Testament, mainly in the Prophets.)

THE ALTAR OF CONSISTENCY. The altar was the place where sacrifices were offered to God for the forgiveness of sins and in response to God's acts of grace and mercy to his people. Amos condemns the people for attempting to offer sacrifices representing repentance (turning from sin) or thanksgiving (praising God for his grace and mercy) while not demonstrating repentance, grace, or mercy in their relationships with others. Such sacrifices demonstrated an inconsistent heart and were, therefore, false worship. Jesus makes the same point in his Sermon on the Mount when he says that worshipers should be reconciled first with those whom they have offended; then, after pursuing reconciliation with others, they may offer their sacrifice at the altar (Matt. 5:23–24). One cannot rightly repent to God while refusing to repent to one he or she has wronged, nor can one rightly give thanks to God for his mercy and grace while refusing to show mercy and grace to others (Matt. 18:21–35).

▶ Theological Soundings

GOD'S SELF-REVELATION. Although God's existence, his power, and even something of his nature can be discerned from creation (Ps. 19:1–6; Rom. 1:19), ultimately God remains beyond our comprehension. He is the creator and sustainer of the universe, and his thoughts and ways are beyond our thoughts and ways (Isa. 55:8–9). The only way for us to know the Lord, to gain understanding about him and his wondrous workings, is for him to stoop down and reveal himself to us (Amos 3:7–8). And in his mercy and kindness God does, in fact, reveal himself to us in his Word.

RESPONDING TO GRACE. God's gift of salvation is free and unmerited; that is, it is not and cannot be earned. It is received by faith alone. However, such receiving faith never remains alone but always responds with a life of thanksgiving. Obedience to God does not earn his favor, grace, or salvation. Rather, good works and obedience to God *respond to* God's favor, grace, and salvation (as in Amos 2:10); they are the means by which we express gratitude and say thank you to God (Rom. 12:1–2). Furthermore, such good works and obedience demonstrate a person's faith, revealing whether they have truly received the free gift of God's salvation and favor (Matt. 7:17–20; James 2:14–26).

Personal Implications

Take time to reflect on the implications of Amos 2:6–3:15 for your own life today. Consider what you have learned that might lead you to praise God, repent of sin, and trust in his gracious promises. Write down your reflections under the three headings we have considered and on the passage as a whole.

1. Gospel Glimpses

2. Whole-Bible Connections

3. Theological Soundings

4. Amos 2:6–3:15

▶ **As You Finish This Unit . . .**

Take a moment now to ask for the Lord's blessing and help as you continue in this study of Joel, Amos, and Obadiah. And take a moment also to look back through this unit of study, to reflect on some key things that the Lord may be teaching you.

Definitions

[1] **Nazirite** – A person set apart for special service to God, which was characterized by a vow that included prohibitions against eating or drinking anything pertaining to the grapevine, cutting or shaving the hair on the head, and touching or even approaching a dead body (See Num. 6:1–21).

[2] **Grace** – Unmerited favor, especially the free gift of salvation that God gives to believers through faith in Jesus Christ.

[3] **Transgression** – A violation of a command or law.

WEEK 7: PREPARE TO MEET YOUR GOD

Amos 4:1–5:17

The Place of the Passage

Amos continues his pronouncement of judgment against Israel, first with a word against the Israelite women. Then the list of crimes includes polluting the worship of God, failing to return to him, and mistreating the poor and powerless in their midst. In light of Israel's sin, Amos warns them to prepare to meet their God (4:12)! But Israel is not without hope; despite such terrible judgment, God still calls his people to turn from evil back to him, to seek him and live, for the Lord may yet be gracious.

The Big Picture

Even amid judgment and tragedy, God still calls his people to return to him and find mercy and grace.

> ## Reflection and Discussion

Read through the complete passage for this study, Amos 4:1–5:17. Then write your reflections on the following questions. (For further background, see the *ESV Study Bible*, pages 1664–1668; available online at www.esv.org.)

1. Multiplying Transgressions (4:1–5; 5:10–13)

In 4:1–5, the Lord specifically addresses the women of Israel. Why is this addressing of the Israelite women significant?

Review 5:10–13. What sins of Israel are listed here?

Bethel and Gilgal were places significant in Israel's history because of their connection to the worship of God. With biting sarcasm in 4:4–5 (see also 5:4–7), the prophet condemns Israelite worship practices. How has their worship become a transgression against God and his law?

How are our worship practices today in danger of becoming transgressions?

2. Return to Me (4:6–5:9, 14–17)

Read 4:6–11 again and list some of the actions God took against Israel.

Why did God do these things to his people? What impact should this have on the reader?

Look again at 4:13 and 5:8–9. How do these verses relate to and inform the call to return to the Lord?

In 5:4–7, what reasons does Amos give for returning to the Lord?

How about in 5:14–15? What reasons does Amos give in these verses for returning to the Lord?

According to those same verses, how does one return to the Lord?

Where in your own life is God calling you to return to him?

Read through the following three sections on *Gospel Glimpses*, *Whole-Bible Connections*, and *Theological Soundings*. Then take time to consider the *Personal Implications* these sections may have for you.

Gospel Glimpses

DESERVING DISASTER. Sometimes, as Amos notes, tragedies and bad events that happen to us are a direct result or consequence of our sin. (However, this is not always the case; see John 9:1–3 and the corresponding notes in the *ESV Study Bible*.) Nevertheless, whether as a consequence for sin or not, tragedies and physical ailments remind us that we will all pass through death and stand before God in judgment. Accordingly, such difficult circumstances call us to repent and return to the Lord. See Luke 13:1–4 and the corresponding notes in the *ESV Study Bible*.

GRACE. Grace is the free, undeserved, and unearned favor of God, demonstrated particularly in his salvation of his people. In Amos 5, God's grace is anticipated by the remnant of Joseph, who hope that God will relent of the announced judgment or relieve them of their suffering during that judgment (v. 15). This grace that delivers God's people from their deserved judgment looks forward to the grace promised in Jesus Christ, by which those who follow him by faith are not treated as their sins deserve but rather receive the free gift of eternal life (Eph. 2:1–10).

Whole-Bible Connections

POLLUTED WORSHIP. The prophets regularly rebuke God's people for the distortions in their worship of God, as Amos does multiple times in this week's passages. Whether it was incorporating the idols and pagan[1] practices of the nations around them, taking advantage of the weak and impoverished and believing such practice was not inconsistent with the worship, or simply using worship as an attempt to manipulate God, the Israelites consistently abused, misused, and polluted the worship of God. New Testament believers are tempted in many of the same ways, including lying to the Holy Spirit (Acts 5:1–11) and showing favoritism to the wealthy (James 2:1–7). Indeed, the book of 1 Corinthians was written, in large part, to address abuses of the Christian worship service by God's people in Corinth. When we see such abuses, our hearts should be stirred up with longing for the day when God's people worship him perfectly in spirit and in truth (John 4:23–24).

REMNANT. In the days of Noah, God's judgment threatened the total annihilation of humanity, but God preserved for himself a small group of those faithful to him (Genesis 6). Similarly, in the days of the prophet Elijah, it seemed that the spread of evil would rid the world completely of God's people, but God told the prophet he had kept 7,000 in Israel who had not turned aside to worship Baal, a false god (1 Kings 19:1–18). Such "remnants" remind us that God always preserves his people, and through that preservation he protects the reputation and glory of his own name. Later in Israel's history, as exile threatened the elimination of both God's people and the glory and reputation of his name, God reminded his people through the prophets that he would save a remnant for himself (see Amos 5:15), a promise that continues to give courage to the church today. God will keep his people and protect his name.

Theological Soundings

THE CREATOR SETS THE RULES. God's creation of all things, especially humanity, is intimately linked to his judgment of humanity (Amos 4:13; compare Isa. 66:1–6; Jer. 10:11–25; Rom. 1:18–23; Rev. 14:7). As the potter has a right to do with his clay as he pleases, so God, as Creator of humanity, has the right and authority to tell us how to live (see Isa. 29:15–16; 45:9–10). As Creator, he sets the rules.

THE WORSHIP OF GOD. The first commandment that God gives to his people after he delivers them out of Egypt is that "you shall have no other gods before me" (Ex. 20:3). He alone is God, and he alone is to be worshiped. Moreover, as God, he determines how and when we will worship him, meaning we are to worship him only as he has prescribed in his Word, not according to our imaginations, inventions, or even preferences (see Amos 5:21–27). Two sons of Aaron, the first high priest[2]—Nadab and Abihu—were struck dead because they offered worship to God in a manner other than that authorized by the Lord (Lev. 10:1–3), and in the New Testament, people were getting sick and even dying because of their abuse of the Lord's Table, or Communion (1 Cor. 11:27–32). God alone determines how and when he will be worshiped.

Personal Implications

Take time to reflect on the implications of Amos 4:1–5:17 for your own life today. Consider what you have learned that might lead you to praise God, repent of sin, and trust in his gracious promises. Write down your reflections under the three headings we have considered and on the passage as a whole.

1. Gospel Glimpses

2. Whole-Bible Connections

---

3. Theological Soundings

---

4. Amos 4:1–5:17

> ## As You Finish This Unit . . .

Take a moment now to ask for the Lord's blessing and help as you continue in this study of Joel, Amos, and Obadiah. And take a moment also to look back through this unit of study, to reflect on some key things that the Lord may be teaching you.

Definitions

[1] **Paganism** – Any belief system that does not acknowledge the God of the Bible as the one true God. Atheism, polytheism, pantheism, animism, and humanism, as well as numerous other religious systems, can all be classified as forms of paganism.

[2] **Priest** – In OT Israel, the priest represented the people before God, and he represented God before the people. Only those descended from Aaron could be priests. Their prescribed duties also included inspecting and receiving sacrifices from the people and overseeing the daily activities and maintenance of the tabernacle or temple.

WEEK 8: THREE WOES

Amos 5:18–6:14

The Place of the Passage

This section of Amos presents the judgment against Israel in the form of three woe oracles. In the first oracle, the Lord condemns the worship of Israel because it is not accompanied by lives that match the people's professed faith: the Israelites do not show concern for the less fortunate around them. The second oracle condemns Israel's complacency and self-confidence, while the third pronounces judgment against Israel for its self-indulgence and lives of luxury built upon the suffering and abuse of others. The section ends with a promise that the wealthy, apathetic, and self-indulgent will be the first carried off into exile.[1]

The Big Picture

This passage calls God's people to trust in him and not themselves, and reminds us that true worship of God includes lives that match our profession of faith.

Reflection and Discussion

Read through the complete passage for this study, Amos 5:18–6:14. Then write your reflections on the following questions. (For further background, see the *ESV Study Bible*, pages 1668–1670; available online at www.esv.org.)

1. Worship without Justice (5:18–27)

Why would the Israelites be anticipating or desiring the day of the Lord?

How would that day turn out to be a surprise for the Israelites?

What are justice and righteousness (see the note on 5:7 in the *ESV Study Bible*)?

The Lord uses very strong language to refer to the Israelites' worship services, words such as "hate" and "despise." Why does God reject their worship?

2. Complacency (6:1–3)

In spite of the disasters that have come upon the surrounding nations (through the Assyrian army; see the note on 6:2 in the *ESV Study Bible*, page 1669), many of whom were larger and stronger than Israel, why do you think the Israelites remain at ease? See also verse 13.

What is the difference between the "ease" of self-confidence and resting in the protection and provision of the Lord?

Where in your life are you at ease in self-confidence? Where do you need to turn and trust in the Lord instead?

3. Self-Indulgence (6:4–14)

Read Amos 3:13–15 again and the note on verse 15 in the ESV *Study Bible*. Are wealth and luxury evil in themselves? Why or why not?

In 6:4–7, what is Israel's crime in regard to their wealth?

How does the punishment of the wealthy fit their crime?

Read through the following three sections on *Gospel Glimpses*, *Whole-Bible Connections*, and *Theological Soundings*. Then take time to consider the *Personal Implications* these sections may have for you.

Gospel Glimpses

SELF-CONFIDENCE. Israel's capital city of Samaria was located on a high hill or mountain, with strong natural defenses. This strategic military position, combined with possible recent military victories in Amos's day, tempted Israel to trust in herself and her strength rather than in the Lord. But salvation comes not in strength or wisdom or riches but in knowing the Lord (Jer. 9:23–24). In fact, the apostle Paul would later say that God chose us not because of our strength or wisdom but because of our weakness and foolishness (1 Cor. 1:26–31); the same was true of Israel (Deut. 7:6–11), but she was quick to forget.

SWEARS BY HIMSELF. Occasionally in the Bible God swears by himself (e.g., Amos 6:8). At first glance, this seems to conflict with Jesus' teaching to let what we say "be simply 'Yes' or 'No'" (Matt. 5:33–37). However, Jesus was addressing a culture in which dishonesty was so rampant that people would excuse away even their oaths and promises based on the precise wording of that by which they swore. For example, they believed an oath sworn by the temple was not binding, but an oath sworn by the gold of the temple *was* binding (see Matt. 23:16–22). Jesus, instead, calls us to such integrity that "yes" means "yes" and "no" means "no." When God swears an oath, it is not because his integrity is in doubt but because he is addressing a people who have become so dishonest that they do not even believe the words of God. And by what should the Lord swear but himself? For there is no one greater (Heb. 6:13–20).

Whole-Bible Connections

EXILE. When God entered into a covenant[2] with his people after delivering them from slavery in Egypt, he promised to bless them for their obedience and to curse them for their disobedience (see Deuteronomy 28). The greatest and final curse was exile (Deut. 28:36–68), in which a foreign nation would come and desolate the cities of Israel and carry the people off as slaves and prisoners to a foreign land. Because of Israel's constant rejection of the Lord, eventually Assyria would come and scatter the northern tribes of Israel (2 Kings 17) and Babylon would eventually come and carry off the southern tribes of Judah into exile (2 Kings 25). However, as we will see, this was not the end of Israel's story.

WOE. A woe oracle is a device used by the prophets to explain the reasons for impending judgment, or to detail that coming judgment, or sometimes both, typically beginning with the announcement formula "Woe to you who . . . ," followed by the oracle. Every prophetic book in the Bible except for Hosea uses this form of judgment announcement. Moreover, Jesus also utilizes this device to announce judgment against the scribes[3] and Pharisees[4] in his day (see Matt. 23:1–36; Luke 11:37–52). We do well ourselves to heed the implicit warnings found in these oracles.

Theological Soundings

JUSTICE. Justice in the Bible includes making right decisions according to God's commands and laws, but it involves much more than legal equity (see Amos 5:24). It denotes, in particular, the fair and just use of power and government to protect the weak and powerless, and it includes individuals' treating one another honestly and fairly, particularly in business practices. To "do justice" is to avoid taking advantage of the poor or those with less access to rights, power, and influence, and to work to protect such members of society. See Jeremiah 22:1–5.

RIGHTEOUSNESS. Righteousness refers to that which is right and proper according to God's norms and moral standards (see Amos 5:24). It refers to doing what is right in God's eyes, especially with regard to our conduct toward others. Justice and righteousness often appear together in Scripture, particularly with reference to the care of those with little or no rights in the ancient Near East, such as orphans, widows, foreigners, and travelers. See James 1:26–27.

Personal Implications

Take time to reflect on the implications of Amos 5:18–6:14 for your own life today. Consider what you have learned that might lead you to praise God, repent of sin, and trust in his gracious promises. Write down your reflections under the three headings we have considered and on the passage as a whole.

1. Gospel Glimpses

2. Whole-Bible Connections

3. Theological Soundings

4. Amos 5:18–6:14

▶ As You Finish This Unit . . .

Take a moment now to ask for the Lord's blessing and help as you continue in this study of Joel, Amos, and Obadiah. And take a moment also to look back through this unit of study, to reflect on some key things that the Lord may be teaching you.

Definitions

[1] **Exile** – Several relocations of large groups of Israelites/Jews have occurred throughout history, but "the exile" typically refers to the Babylonian exile, that is, Nebuchadnezzar's relocation of residents of the southern kingdom of Judah to Babylon in 586 BC. (Residents of the northern kingdom of Israel had been resettled by Assyria in 722 BC.) After Babylon came under Persian rule, several waves of Jewish exiles returned and repopulated Judah.

[2] **Covenant** – A binding agreement between two parties, typically involving a formal statement of their relationship, a list of stipulations and obligations for both parties, a list of witnesses to the agreement, and a list of curses for unfaithfulness and blessings for faithfulness to the agreement. The OT is more properly understood as the old covenant, meaning the agreement established between God and his people prior to the coming of Jesus Christ and the establishment of the new covenant (NT).

[3] **Scribe** – Someone trained and authorized to transcribe, teach, and interpret the Scriptures. Jesus often criticized scribes for their pride, their legalistic approach to the Scriptures, and their refusal to believe in him.

[4] **Pharisee** – A member of a popular religious/political party in NT times characterized by strict adherence to the law of Moses and also to extrabiblical Jewish traditions. The Pharisees were frequently criticized by Jesus for their legalistic and hypocritical practices. The apostle Paul was a zealous Pharisee prior to his conversion.

WEEK 9: TWO VISIONS

Amos 7:1–8:14

The Place of the Passage

The book of Amos closes with three sections of visions. The first consists of three smaller visions through which Amos and God dialogue as Amos prays for Israel and the Lord shows mercy. However, the people persist in their rebellion, and Amos no longer asks the Lord to relent of his judgment. This persistence in rebellion is demonstrated by the priest Amaziah, who rebukes Amos for his harsh words, preferring prophecies of blessing and success instead. The second vision reinforces the coming judgment, as the final harvest has come and the people must reap what they have sown.

The Big Picture

God is patient and slow to anger, waiting for his people to come back to him; even so, the Lord will eventually punish those who persist in their rejection of him.

> ### Reflection and Discussion

Read through the complete passage for this study, Amos 7:1–8:14. Then write your reflections on the following questions. (For further background, see the *ESV Study Bible*, pages 1671–1673; available online at www.esv.org.)

1. The First Visions (7:1–9)

As Amos describes the first two visions he receives from the Lord, there is a back-and-forth between Amos and God. First, God shows Amos the vision; then, Amos intercedes[1] for Israel; accordingly, God relents of the promised judgment. What does this back and forth reveal about Amos?

What does this dialogue reveal about God? See also Exodus 34:6.

What does this dialogue teach us about prayer?

The third time in this passage that God shows Amos a vision, there is no intercession and no relenting of the disaster. Why does Amos not intercede this third time?

What does this third vision, with no relenting, teach us?

2. An Accusing Aside (7:10–17)

How does Amaziah's position as a priest inform our understanding of the spiritual pollution occurring in Israel?

Why do Amaziah and the king want Amos to go away? What messages do they want to hear instead?

Read 2 Timothy 4:1–4. Where do you see "itching ears" today? How are your own ears "itching"?

3. The Second Vision (8:1–14)

List some of the specific ways in which the wealthy in Amos's day were taking advantage of the poor and weak.

Where do you see similar practices occurring in the church today?

How are these abuses of the poor and needy a violation of the Sabbath and the new moon[2] festivals?

Read 8:11–12 again. Why is this famine more difficult and scary than other kinds of famine?

Read through the following three sections on *Gospel Glimpses*, *Whole-Bible Connections*, and *Theological Soundings*. Then take time to consider the *Personal Implications* these sections may have for you.

Gospel Glimpses

THE PATIENCE OF GOD. When Moses asks to see God in Exodus 34, the Lord describes himself as "merciful and gracious, slow to anger, and abounding in steadfast love and faithfulness" (Ex. 34:6). It is this patience and slowness to anger that calls us to turn back to God and away from our sin, from our wandering, and from our rebellion. He is not slow, not reluctant or hesitant to keep his promises of judgment on the wicked and the bringing about of the new age; rather, he is patient, giving time for his people to turn to him in faith and repentance (2 Pet. 3:9).

AN END TO SECOND CHANCES. Although God is patient, slow to anger, and forbearing for us to return to him, there is an end to his patience. In Exodus 34:7, God "[forgives] iniquity[3] and transgression and sin," but he does not "clear the guilty." Jesus shares a parable about the end of second chances in Luke 16:19–31, reminding us that, after death, we will all face judgment (Heb. 9:27), and there will no longer be an opportunity to repent and turn back to the Lord.

Whole-Bible Connections

PERSECUTING THE PROPHETS. Throughout the Bible, God's messengers are often persecuted. In the Old Testament, the prophets who were faithful to preach God's truth, even when it was not pleasant, were often rejected or ridiculed and even suffered physical harm. The disciples of Jesus suffered the same kinds of persecution, including beatings, stonings, and imprisonments, and

Jesus himself suffered rejection and persecution, even from those who professed faith in God. Furthermore, Jesus promises such hardships for all who follow him: the world will hate followers of Jesus and those who faithfully proclaim his life, ministry, death, resurrection, and teachings, because the world hates Jesus himself (John 15:18–25; see also Matt. 5:10–12 and 10:16–23).

SABBATH FOR THE POOR. When God gave his law to the Israelites after he rescued them from slavery in Egypt, he specified that, in the observance of the Sabbath, all people were to rest. Exodus 20:10 notes that no one shall work, including "your son, or your daughter, your male servant, or your female servant, . . . or the sojourner who is within your gates." The Sabbath regulations particularly protect the poor, because they are the most likely to have to work every day of the week. In the ancient world, there was no rest for the slave or the servant, and there were no breaks for the poor; only the wealthy could afford days of leisure and rest. The same remains true today; it is the wealthy who can afford to take one day out of seven for rest and worship, while the poor work two and sometimes three jobs, usually working every day of the week. Moreover, it is the service industries with lower-wage workers, such as restaurants and retail stores, that stay open seven days a week. But God's day of rest is for all people, regardless of their socioeconomic status; in fact, it seems that the Sabbath was designed, in part, specifically to protect those of lower socioeconomic status.

Theological Soundings

PRAYER. God answers prayer. He is near to his people, and his ear is attentive to their pleas. Prayer matters, and prayer has effects. For example, Jesus promises to answer prayer (John 14:12–14), and James promises that "the prayer of a righteous person has great power" (James 5:16–18). Therefore, God in his Word regularly calls us to pray: for our churches and each other (Eph. 6:18–20), for the gospel as it goes forth (Matt. 9:35–38; 2 Thess. 3:1–5), and even for our enemies (Matt. 5:43–48). Indeed, we are to pray for all people, praying especially that they may come to know the Lord (1 Tim. 2:1–7).

ACCOUNTABILITY. Throughout the books of the prophets in the Old Testament, it often seems that God's harshest rebukes are for his priests and teachers. The same is true of the spiritual leaders in Jesus' day: Christ's harshest rebukes are often directed at the Pharisees, Sadducees, and teachers of the law. With greater knowledge comes greater accountability, and those to whom much has been entrusted, from them will more be demanded (see Luke 12:41–48). James reminds us, "Not many of you should become teachers, . . . for you know that we who teach will be judged with greater strictness" (James 3:1).

Personal Implications

Take time to reflect on the implications of Amos 7:1–8:14 for your own life today. Consider what you have learned that might lead you to praise God, repent of sin, and trust in his gracious promises. Write down your reflections under the three headings we have considered and on the passage as a whole.

1. Gospel Glimpses

2. Whole-Bible Connections

3. Theological Soundings

4. Amos 7:1–8:14

As You Finish This Unit . . .

Take a moment now to ask for the Lord's blessing and help as you continue in this study of Joel, Amos, and Obadiah. And take a moment also to look back through this unit of study, to reflect on some key things that the Lord may be teaching you.

Definitions

[1] **Intercession** – Appealing to one person on behalf of another. Often used with reference to prayer.

[2] **New moon** – In Israel, a monthly celebration that was to be a time of spiritual renewal coinciding with the monthly new moon. It was a time of gathering together, waiting on the Lord, and hearing from him.

[3] **Iniquity** – Any violation of or failure to adhere to the commands of God, or the desire to do so.

Week 10: One All-Powerful, Ever-Present Judge

Amos 9:1–15

The Place of the Passage

The book of Amos ends with one more vision from the Lord. In this vision, Amos sees God standing beside the altar, and he hears both a message of judgment and a message of hope. In the message of judgment, God reminds Amos of his eternal presence and that the wicked cannot hide from him. Then, in the final word through the prophet Amos, God assures his people that he will preserve them and that a day is coming in which he will gather all of his people from the ends of the earth. On that day, the people of God will dwell in safety forever.

The Big Picture

The wicked cannot hide from God's judgment, but the people of God can hope in God's restoration.

Reflection and Discussion

Read through the complete passage for this study, Amos 9:1–15. Then write your reflections on the following questions. (For further background, see the *ESV Study Bible*, pages 1674–1675; available online at www.esv.org.)

1. A Last Vision (9:1–10)

Read Psalm 139:7–12. In this psalm, the omnipresence of God is a source of comfort and strength to the psalmist. In Amos 9:2–4, this omnipresence is turned against Israel in judgment. How does God's omnipresence enhance or heighten the judgment against Israel?

How do verses 5–6 paint a picture of the power of God? How is this power linked to the judgment proclaimed by Amos?

The Cushites were regarded as living at the far end of the world. Why does God liken his special people Israel to the Cushites?

Israel believed that, since they were God's chosen people, they would forever remain under his divine protection, regardless of how they lived: "Disaster shall not overtake or meet us" (v. 10). In reality, their status as God's chosen people resulted in a greater accountability and higher standard for them (vv. 7–10). How do we presume upon God today? How do God's people today act as if "Disaster shall not overtake or meet us"?

2. A Lasting Hope (9:11–15)

When the nation of Israel divided into two kingdoms, Israel in the north and Judah in the south, the northern kingdom's first king, Jeroboam, was afraid that people would continue to worship in Jerusalem at the temple, which was in the southern kingdom. He feared that such regular pilgrimages to Jerusalem would reunite the nation of Israel by turning the heart of the people in the north back toward the city and temple in Jerusalem and back toward the descendants of beloved King David. In order to protect his reign over the northern part of Israel, Jeroboam made his own cities of worship and even created his own annual worship festival, patterned after Judah's festival of booths[1] and even celebrated around the same time of year (see 1 Kings 12:25–33). In light of this background, how might the Israelites hear the promise that hope will come through the "booth of David" (Amos 9:11)?

A "booth" is a temporary shelter, such as those the Israelites might have inhabited when they first came out of Egypt and were making their way toward the Promised Land (see Lev. 23:33–43). Why do you think God uses something so fragile as the symbol of his promised salvation?

Read 1 Corinthians 1:18–25. How does God's use of something as fragile as a booth to symbolize salvation inform your understanding of the "foolishness of God" in 1 Corinthians 1:18–25? How is the cross like the booth mentioned in Amos 9:11–15?

Edom is often used by the prophets as a representative of those hostile to the people of God. In fact, one of the most violent and difficult psalms is Psalm 137, in which God's people plead with God for vengeance against Edom. Even the book of Amos begins with an oracle against Edom. Take a moment to reread that oracle in Amos 1:11–12. What, then, is the hope that God promises in 9:12?

How should it impact the church to see that the Lord will save even some people previously hostile to him and his people?

The book of Amos ends with the promise of a day coming for God's people, a day of hope and security. Using the concepts of Amos 9:13–15, describe that coming day in your own words. What exactly is God promising to his people on that coming day?

Read through the following three sections on *Gospel Glimpses*, *Whole-Bible Connections*, and *Theological Soundings*. Then take time to consider the *Personal Implications* these sections may have for you.

Gospel Glimpses

GOD'S POWER IN WEAKNESS. The psalmist declares, "Some trust in chariots and some in horses, but we trust in the name of the LORD our God" (Ps. 20:7). The world prizes strength, riches, and wisdom, but God's salvation and help often come to us in the form of weakness, even something as insignificant as a "booth" (Amos 9:11). For example, God had Gideon whittle down his army until it was so small that victory seemed impossible, so that the credit for victory would go to God alone (Judg. 7:1–8). God commanded kings in Israel not to amass horses—which were essential for military conquest—so that they would rely on God's strength and power, not their own (Deut. 17:16). And in the New Testament, the apostle Paul reminds us that God's power "is made perfect in weakness," and Paul, therefore, boasts in his weakness and not in his strength (2 Cor. 12:1–10). Our weaknesses help us rely more and more on the strength of God, and "boasting in our weakness" is a turning away from self-reliance and self-sufficiency to dependence upon the Lord.

THE FOOLISHNESS OF THE CROSS. Perhaps nowhere as clearly as at the cross of Jesus Christ does the power and wisdom of God appear as weakness and foolishness to the world (see the comments above on Amos 9:11–15). What victory could possibly come from the apparent defeat at the hands of the Jews and Romans at Jesus' arrest and trial? What glory could possibly come through such humiliation as being crucified like a criminal? What power could possibly come from the weakness of a torturous and suffocating death on a cross? It is for these reasons, among others, that the cross is a "stumbling block to Jews and folly to Gentiles" (1 Cor. 1:23). The cross is foolishness to the world but wisdom and power to those who trust in it for salvation.

▶ Whole-Bible Connections

THE BOOTH OF DAVID. Used only in this week's passage and in James' quote of the passage in Acts 15:14–18, the revival of the "booth of David" indicates the hope of God's people in the restoration of Israel through a descendant of King David. God promised David that one of his descendants would reign over God's people forever (2 Sam. 7:12–17), and Israel was reminded of that hope particularly through the prophets by such references as the "Branch" (Jer. 23:5; 33:15), the "shoot" (Isa. 11:1), and the "booth" of David. For Israel, this became hope in a return to the glory days of King David, when Israel experienced expansion of their land, unification of their nation, and peace[2] from their enemies. Ultimately, however, these hopes point to a hope in the coming Savior, the Lord Jesus Christ, who would bring about the spiritual and eternal kingdom of God, ultimate victory over God's enemies, and eternal peace for his people.

SALVATION FOR THE NATIONS. From God's first call to Abraham, it has always been the Lord's plan to bring salvation to all nations on earth. God's promise to Abraham was that he would be a blessing, so that in him "all the families of the earth shall be blessed" (Gen. 12:3). That was the mission of Israel: to proclaim the light of salvation to all nations. And it is the hope proclaimed by the prophets, that at the end of time God would gather his people from all nations on earth (Isa. 66:18–23). Although we see a glimpse of the gathering of the nations in the Old Testament through the faith of such non-Israelites as Rahab and Ruth, the expansion of the gospel to the nations is seen most clearly in the book of Acts. In fact, James quotes the hope of Amos 9:11–12 in his speech at the first council meeting of church leaders in Jerusalem in defense of Gentile followers of Jesus (Acts 15:12–21). This expansion of the gospel to the ends of the earth anticipates that great and glorious day when people from every nation, tribe, people, and language gather to worship the Lord together in eternity (Rev. 7:9).

▶ Theological Soundings

OMNIPRESENCE. God is a spirit and therefore does not have spatial dimensions. He is present everywhere at all times with his whole being. This means that God's people can seek him anywhere, no matter where they are, and it means that we are never alone. God truly is always with us and always near us, and we are always safely in his hands. For those who do not love God or follow him, however, there is nothing they can hide from God, nor anywhere they can run from God (Amos 9:2–4). For the wicked, there is no place safe from God (Jer. 23:23–24).

OMNIPOTENCE. God is all-powerful and able to do everything he wills (see Amos 9:5–6). This means that God's desires and ultimate will are never thwarted, prevented, or frustrated by his enemies. He alone executes his perfect plan. That means we can rest in his power, trusting that his plans will never be stopped and his kingdom will never be defeated. God always keeps his promises, because he alone has the power to ensure that they are fulfilled (Isa. 14:27).

Personal Implications

Take time to reflect on the implications of Amos 9:1–15 for your own life today. Consider what you have learned that might lead you to praise God, repent of sin, and trust in his gracious promises. Write down your reflections under the three headings we have considered and on the passage as a whole.

1. Gospel Glimpses

2. Whole-Bible Connections

3. Theological Soundings

4. Amos 9:1–15

> ### As You Finish This Unit . . .

Take a moment now to ask for the Lord's blessing and help as you continue in this study of Joel, Amos, and Obadiah. And take a moment also to look back through this unit of study, to reflect on some key things that the Lord may be teaching you.

Definitions

[1] **Festival of Booths** – An annual festival in Israel that both celebrated the end of the harvest and also commemorated God's deliverance of his people at the exodus. The people would often spend seven days in temporary structures called "booths" to remember the journey out of Egypt.

[2] **Peace** – In modern use, the absence of tension or conflict. In biblical use, a condition of well-being or wholeness that God grants his people, which also results in harmony with God and others.

Week 11: The Kingdom Shall Be the Lord's

Obadiah

The Place of the Passage

In the book of Obadiah, God promises through his prophet to bring judgment upon Edom. When Babylon invaded Israel and carried off God's people into exile, not only did Edom fail to help Israel—she helped Babylon instead. Moreover, Edom seemed to revel in the destruction of Israel. Therefore, God is bringing judgment against Edom, and that judgment in the book of Obadiah comes with a promise of final restoration for God's people, when a Savior will ultimately deliver and rule over them.

The Big Picture

Obadiah anticipates the kingdom of the Lord by proclaiming judgment against Edom and the eventual salvation and restoration of Israel.

Reflection and Discussion

Read through the complete passage for this study, Obadiah 1–21. Then write your reflections on the following questions. (For further background, see the *ESV Study Bible*, pages 1680–1682; available online at www.esv.org.)

1. Judgment on Edom (1–14)

Edom was located in a mountainous region, making it difficult for foreign armies to invade and thus giving Edom a sense of invincibility, of security and safety. How is this sense of security exaggerated in the first few verses of Obadiah (vv. 3–4)?

Despite Edom's perception of safety, God is bringing destruction upon the nation. What is the reason for this judgment against Edom? What has Edom done to Israel?

What was Edom's response to Israel's destruction at the hand of Babylon?

How do thieves and grape-gatherers provide a picture of Edom's total destruction? How is this a fitting punishment for Edom?

From where will this punishment on Edom come (v. 1)? How will God bring his judgment against Edom?

---

2. Comfort for Israel (15–21)

The oracles against foreign nations are sometimes given to those nations about whom destruction is proclaimed (for example, the book of Jonah, where judgment against Nineveh is proclaimed in Nineveh by Jonah) and sometimes proclaimed in the presence of ambassadors visiting the royal court of Israel. However, the audience for such oracles is also—if not primarily—the people of God, and these oracles eventually become part of God's Word for his people. Why does God include such oracles against foreign nations in his message to his people?

What purpose might this oracle against Edom serve for the people of Israel, who suffered because of Edom?

How does this purpose give God's people hope today? What do such oracles against foreign nations in the Bible offer to God's people today?

The geographic references in verses 19–20 suggest the outermost boundaries of the original Promised Land, most of which has been conquered by foreign armies and is inhabited by foreign nations. What, then, is the hope offered to Israel at the end of Obadiah?

Read Revelation chapter 21. How does the hope of Obadiah 19–21 translate to believers after the first coming of Christ?

How does Obadiah 21 point to Jesus?

Read through the following three sections on *Gospel Glimpses, Whole-Bible Connections*, and *Theological Soundings*. Then take time to consider the *Personal Implications* these sections may have for you.

Gospel Glimpses

SAVIORS. Obadiah 21 promises that saviors will come to deliver and rule over God's people, and such promises permeate the Old Testament. For example, in the book of Judges, when God's people turn to him in their distress because of the oppression of foreign nations, God raises up saviors, or "judges," who deliver and rule over his people. Later, at the end of the exile in Babylon, God raises up Cyrus the Persian, who defeats Babylon and releases the Jews to return back to the land of Israel, thereby bringing an end to the exile. Cyrus, then, is a kind of savior who delivers God's people. Each of these "saviors" in the Old Testament anticipates the one true and final Savior, Jesus Christ, who will ultimately deliver God's people from the enemies of sin and death and will rule over them as King of kings and Lord of lords (Rev. 19:11–16).

THE APPLE OF HIS EYE. Obadiah's oracle against Edom reveals God's special and tender love for his people, because Edom's judgment is specifically linked to Edom's mistreatment of God's people. Throughout the Bible we see this special love that God has for his people. For example, Deuteronomy 32:10–14 details God's rescue of his people, his caring for them, and his keeping them "as the apple of his eye." Hosea 11 describes God's calling of his people out of Egypt in terms of a father teaching his son to walk. And Isaiah 43 notes God's protective presence and deep affection for his people (Isa. 43:1–7). Likewise, the New Testament revels in this same deep affection, the love that God lavishes upon his people through Jesus Christ (Eph. 2:4; 3:14–19; 1 John 3:1), a love from which nothing can separate us (Rom. 8:31–39).

Whole-Bible Connections

THE CITY OF GOD. Before Israel existed as a people, God brought Abraham to the land of Canaan and promised that one day his people would dwell in that land as a great nation (Gen. 12:4–7). Eventually, God's people would indeed occupy that land, and God would establish a temporary, earthly kingdom, with a capital at Jerusalem standing as the city of God. However, it was never God's plan for that physical, earthly city to be the permanent kingdom of God's people. In fact, the author of Hebrews notes that even Abraham, long before the physical city of Jerusalem existed, was looking forward "to the city that has foundations, whose designer and builder is God" (Heb. 11:10; see also vv. 13–16). The hope of God's people, then, is for an eternal, spiritual city, the new Jerusalem that God will bring at the end of time (Revelation 21; compare Obad. 21).

THE CUP OF THE LORD'S WRATH. Throughout the Bible, the wrath of God is imaged as a cup of wine that, when drunk, does not bring the joy and delight of good wine but rather brings pain, misery, judgment, and destruction (Obad. 16). Most prominently, in Jeremiah 25:15–29 the Lord instructs the prophet Jeremiah to make all of the nations drink his "cup of the wine of wrath" (v. 15), which will be as a sword against them. Jesus uses this same image in his prayer in the garden (Matt. 26:36–46), which anticipates his bearing the wrath of God that we deserve for our sins. Instead of our drinking that deserved wine of God's wrath, Jesus drinks it on our behalf, paying the penalty we deserve on the cross.

However, for those who do not follow Jesus by faith, the cup of wrath remains for them to drink in judgment at the end of time (Rev. 14:9–11).

Theological Soundings

DIRECTING THE NATIONS. The book of Obadiah opens with the Lord's summoning the nations to war against Edom. This summons reminds us that God "rules over the nations" (Ps. 22:28). He raises up rulers and builds up nations and also deposes rulers and tears down nations (Job 12:23; Isa. 41:2; Jer. 1:9–10). Moreover, as we see in Obadiah, God uses the nations to accomplish his purposes and to provide for, protect, discipline, and deliver his people.

THE UNIVERSAL KINGDOM OF GOD. The "kingdom of God" is a broad term used to describe both God's universal rule over all things, places, and people, and also his rule over his particular people. As a term for God's universal rule over all things, places, and people, God reigns as sovereign ruler over the universe (Ps. 103:19; Dan. 4:35), even though, for a time, he has allowed the Enemy, the Devil,[1] to have some power with which to build his own kingdom of darkness. That power of the Enemy, however, remains a limited power and for a limited time.

THE PARTICULAR KINGDOM OF GOD. The "kingdom of God" as a reference to God's rule over his particular people refers to God's plan to use his people to advance the good news of his salvation and to push back the power and influence of the kingdom of darkness. This particular people was, in the Old Testament, represented visibly through the nation or kingdom of Israel. However, as God's plan continued to be unveiled, it became more and more clear that the weapons of the kingdom were not military or political but rather spiritual, and with the first coming of Jesus Christ, God revealed fully that his kingdom was a spiritual kingdom and that the advancement of the kingdom was a spiritual advancement (John 18:36; Eph. 6:10–20). Furthermore, though Jesus declared that the kingdom has come and is already here (Matt. 12:28; Luke 17:20–21), he also taught us to pray for the kingdom to come (Matt. 6:10), demonstrating that the kingdom has both an "already" and a "not yet" aspect. The kingdom of God, then, is King Jesus bringing about his rule over all things, not with military or political power but by his Holy Spirit working through his people, who eagerly await the return of the King and the fullness of his kingdom.

Personal Implications

Take time to reflect on the implications of Obadiah 1–21 for your own life today. Consider what you have learned that might lead you to praise God, repent of sin, and trust in his gracious promises. Write down your reflections under the three headings we have considered and on the passage as a whole.

1. Gospel Glimpses

2. Whole-Bible Connections

3. Theological Soundings

4. Obadiah 1–21

▶ As You Finish This Unit . . .

Take a moment now to ask for the Lord's blessing and help as we conclude our study of Joel, Amos, and Obadiah. And take a moment also to look back through this unit of study, to reflect on some key things that the Lord may be teaching you.

Definition

[1] **Satan/the Devil** – A spiritual being whose name means "accuser." As the leader of all the demonic forces, he opposes God's rule and seeks to harm God's people and accuse them of wrongdoing. His power, however, is confined to the bounds that God has set for him, and one day he will be destroyed along with all his demons (Matt. 25:41; Rev. 20:10).

WEEK 12: SUMMARY AND CONCLUSION

We conclude our study of Joel, Amos, and Obadiah by summarizing the big picture of God's message through these books. Then we will consider several questions in order to reflect on various Gospel Glimpses, Whole-Bible Connections, and Theological Soundings throughout the entire study.

The Big Picture of Joel, Amos, and Obadiah

Joel, Amos, and Obadiah all anticipate the day of the Lord. In that day, God will first judge his own people for their sin and rebellion, holding them to a higher standard because they have received the Word of God. Next, that day will bring judgment upon the nations. The nations will be judged not only for their treatment of God's people but also for whether they adhered to the laws and ways of God, which are plainly evident in creation.

Nevertheless, despite the judgment accompanying the day of the Lord, it will be a day of hope for God's people. On that day, God will firmly establish his rule over all nations and will vindicate his people through the exercise of his justice. That day, then, will ultimately be a day of renewal in which the shame and reproach of God's people will be removed and what was once lost will be fully restored in abundance.

Joel's anticipation of the day of the Lord begins with the people's lament over a devastating locust plague, which Joel uses to illustrate the devastation that the coming judgment, through an enemy army coming from the north, will bring upon Israel. However, if God's people repent and turn back to God, rending their hearts before him, he will come and destroy that invading army and bring about a time of refreshment for his people. In that time, the shame of God's people will be removed, the years the locust ate will be restored, and, more importantly, the people will be reconciled to their God, a reconciliation anticipating the future day in which God will pour out his Holy Spirit upon all who call on his name. The book of Joel ends with the anticipation of the day of the Lord, in which God will bring judgment upon the nations, that is, upon those who are God's enemies and the enemies of his people.

Amos, conversely, *begins* with the judgment of the nations. However, after building the joyful anticipation of Israel over the destruction of their enemies, Amos turns suddenly and proclaims that Israel, too, will be subject to God's judgment. Through a series of four oracles and two visions, Amos denounces Israel's false worship, because the people neglect daily justice and righteousness; he also denounces their complacency, arrogance, and self-indulgence, especially their extravagance at the expense of the weak and impoverished. Even so, the day of the Lord is an object of hope for God's people, and the book of Amos ends with a third vision through which God promises to raise up the booth of David, to gather his people from every nation, and to protect them from ever again being uprooted. That day will be one of such blessing from God that the land itself will overflow with abundant provisions from him.

The day of the Lord in the book of Obadiah concentrates on God's judgment against Edom for participating and reveling in the destruction of God's people by Babylon's army. This judgment will bring about the vindication of God's people for the evil done to them by Edom. Although Obadiah is a very short book focusing on God's judgment against Edom, it also contains the hopeful aspect of the day of the Lord through Obadiah's anticipation of the rule of the King over all nations.

Throughout Israel's history, glimpses can be seen of the fulfillment of that promised day of the Lord. For example, with Cyrus's decree in 538 BC, the Jews exiled to Babylon were granted permission to return to the Promised Land and to begin rebuilding their lives. The defeat of Babylon and the return to the land were a partial fulfillment of the day of the Lord and a glimpse of what was yet to come. However, the people were still awaiting the complete fulfillment of the prophetic promise. Obadiah notes that saviors shall go up to Mount Zion, and in the fullness of time the one final Savior, Jesus Christ, would come and be lifted up for the salvation of his people. And one day, Jesus will return for the final day of the Lord, as King of kings and Lord of lords. On that great day, everyone will give an answer for his or her deeds, beginning with the people of God. And then, after the judgment of the nations, God's people will dwell with him forever, "And they shall never again be uprooted" (Amos 9:15).

Gospel Glimpses

Joel, Amos, and Obadiah each anticipate God's judgment of all people, but these books also promise the forgiveness and restoration of God's people. How is that forgiveness possible? Only through the blood of Jesus Christ. Indeed, as Obadiah anticipates, a Savior would come who would defeat the true enemies of God's people: sin, death, and the powers of darkness. Through the resurrection of Jesus Christ, God's people know victory over the enemies of sin, death, and darkness in this life; but ultimately, like the people in the time of Joel, Amos, and Obadiah, we await a future day of the Lord in which the Savior will return, vindicate his people, and establish finally his complete rule over all the nations.

How have Joel, Amos, and Obadiah brought new clarity to your understanding of the gospel?

What particular passages or themes in Joel, Amos, or Obadiah have led you to have a fresh understanding and grasp of God's grace to us through Jesus?

Whole-Bible Connections

Israel in the time of these prophets had presumed upon the grace of God, believing that since they had a special relationship with God, they could live however they wanted. But Joel, Amos, and Obadiah remind us that God's people are held to a higher standard before the judgment of God precisely because we have received God's Word and have experienced a relationship with him. This gracious standing with God obligates us to live in a manner worthy of the calling we have received (Eph. 4:1–3), and we will be judged according to how we respond to the gracious blessings of God (James 2:12). Nevertheless, this discipline is also a demonstration of God's faithful love for his people (Heb. 12:3–11), and even in the midst of such judgment, we can hold fast to God's promise of a coming day of vindication, salvation, and restoration.

How has this study of Joel, Amos, and Obadiah filled out your understanding of the biblical storyline of redemption?

What themes emphasized in Joel, Amos, and Obadiah have helped you deepen your grasp of the Bible's unity?

What passages or themes have expanded your understanding of the redemption that Jesus provides, begun at his first coming and to be consummated at his return?

What connections between these books and the New Testament were new to you?

Theological Soundings

Through these three books of the Bible, we have learned much about God, including his omnipotence, his omnipresence, and his sovereignty, demonstrated especially in his rule over the nations. We have also learned much about what God expects of us: right worship, a proper response to grace, appreciation of the power and role of prayer, and a desire for justice and righteousness. Additionally, we have seen God's love for humanity through the dignity he gives to all those made in his image, and also the Lord's vindication of his particular people and the revenge he brings against his and our enemies. Further, we have explored the universal offer of salvation to all who call on the name of the Lord, and the reality that those who answer that call do so only because the Lord has called them to salvation.

How has your theology been refined during the course of studying Joel, Amos, and Obadiah?

How has your understanding of the nature and character of God been deepened throughout this study?

What unique contributions do Joel, Amos, and Obadiah make toward our understanding of who Jesus is and what he accomplished through his life, death, and resurrection?

What specifically do Joel, Amos, and Obadiah teach us about the human condition and our need of redemption?

Personal Implications

God gave us the books of Joel, Amos, and Obadiah, ultimately, to transform us into the likeness of his Son. If our study of these prophets does not strengthen our communion with God and worship of him, we have been wasting our time. As you reflect on our study of Joel, Amos, and Obadiah as a whole, what implications do you see for your own life?

What life implications flow from your reflections on the questions already asked in this week's study concerning Gospel Glimpses, Whole-Bible Connections, and Theological Soundings from the entire book?

What have these books brought home to you that leads you to praise God, turn away from sin, and trust more firmly in his promises?

As You Finish Studying Joel, Amos, and Obadiah . . .

We rejoice with you as you finish studying the books of Joel, Amos, and Obadiah! May this study become part of your Christian walk of faith, day by day and week by week throughout all your life. Now we would greatly encourage you to study the Word of God in an ongoing way. To help you as you continue your study of the Bible, we would encourage you to consider other books in the *Knowing the Bible* series, and to visit www.knowingthebibleseries.org.

Lastly, take a moment to look back through this study. Review the notes that you have written, and the things that you have highlighted or underlined. Reflect again on the key themes that the Lord has been teaching you about himself and about his Word. May these things become a treasure for you throughout your life—this we pray in the name of the Father, and the Son, and the Holy Spirit. Amen.